C000174295

P

by Iain Gray

Lang**Syne**

PUBLISHING

WRITING *to* REMEMBER

WRITING *to* REMEMBER

79 Main Street, Newtongrange,
Midlothian EH22 4NA
Tel: 0131 344 0414   Fax: 0845 075 6085
E-mail: info@lang-syne.co.uk
www.langsyneshop.co.uk

Design by Dorothy Meikle
Printed by Printwell Ltd
© Lang Syne Publishers Ltd 2019

ISBN 978-1-85217-539-9

Palmer

MOTTO:
The palm is for virtue.

CREST:
A hand grasping a palmer's staff.

NAME variations include:
Pallmer
Parmer

Chapter one:

The origins of popular surnames

by George Forbes and Iain Gray

If you don't know where you came from, you won't know where you're going is a frequently quoted observation and one that has a particular resonance today when there has been a marked upsurge in interest in genealogy, with increasing numbers of people curious to trace their family roots.

Main sources for genealogical research include census returns and official records of births, marriages and deaths – and the key to unlocking the detail they contain is obviously a family surname, one that has been 'inherited' and passed from generation to generation.

No matter our station in life, we all have a surname – but it was not until about the middle of the fourteenth century that the practice of being identified by a particular surname became commonly established throughout the British Isles.

Previous to this, it was normal for a person to be identified through the use of only a forename.

But as population gradually increased and there were many more people with the same forename, surnames were adopted to distinguish one person, or community, from another.

Many common English surnames are patronymic in origin, meaning they stem from the forename of one's father – with 'Johnson,' for example, indicating 'son of John.'

It was the Normans, in the wake of their eleventh century conquest of Anglo-Saxon England, a pivotal moment in the nation's history, who first brought surnames into usage – although it was a gradual process.

For the Normans, these were names initially based on the title of their estates, local villages and chateaux in France to distinguish and identify these landholdings.

Such grand descriptions also helped enhance the prestige of these warlords and generally glorify their lofty positions high above the humble serfs slaving away below in the pecking order who had only single names, often with Biblical connotations as in Pierre and Jacques.

The only descriptive distinctions among the peasantry concerned their occupations, like 'Pierre the swineherd' or 'Jacques the ferryman.'

Roots of surnames that came into usage in England not only included Norman-French, but also Old French, Old Norse, Old English, Middle English, German, Latin, Greek, Hebrew and the Gaelic languages of the Celts.

The Normans themselves were originally Vikings, or 'Northmen', who raided, colonised and eventually settled down around the French coastline.

The had sailed up the Seine in their longboats in 900AD under their ferocious leader Rollo and ruled the roost in north eastern France before sailing over to conquer England in 1066 under Duke William of Normandy – better known to posterity as William the Conqueror, or King William I of England.

Granted lands in the newly-conquered England, some of their descendants later acquired territories in Wales, Scotland and Ireland – taking not only their own surnames, but also the practice of adopting a surname, with them.

But it was in England where Norman rule and custom first impacted, particularly in relation to the adoption of surnames.

This is reflected in the famous *Domesday Book*, a massive survey of much of England and Wales, ordered by William I, to determine who owned what, what it was worth and therefore how much they were liable to pay in taxes to the voracious Royal Exchequer.

Completed in 1086 and now held in the National Archives in Kew, London, 'Domesday' was an Old English word meaning 'Day of Judgement.'

This was because, in the words of one contemporary chronicler, "its decisions, like those of the Last Judgement, are unalterable."

It had been a requirement of all those English landholders – from the richest to the poorest – that they identify themselves for the purposes of the survey and for future reference by means of a surname.

This is why the *Domesday Book*, although written in Latin as was the practice for several centuries with both civic and ecclesiastical records, is an invaluable source for the early appearance of a wide range of English surnames.

Several of these names were coined in connection with occupations.

These include Baker and Smith, while Cooks, Chamberlains, Constables and Porters were to be found carrying out duties in large medieval households.

The church's influence can be found in names such as Bishop, Friar and Monk while the popular name of Bennett derives from the late fifth to mid-sixth century Saint Benedict, founder of the Benedictine order of monks.

The early medical profession is represented by Barber, while businessmen produced names that include Merchant and Sellers.

Down at the village watermill, the names that cropped up included Millar/Miller, Walker and Fuller, while other self-explanatory trades included Cooper, Tailor, Mason and Wright.

Even the scenery was utilised as in Moor, Hill, Wood and Forrest – while the hunt and the chase supplied names that include Hunter, Falconer, Fowler and Fox.

Colours are also a source of popular surnames, as in Black, Brown, Gray/Grey, Green and White, and would have denoted the colour of the clothing the person habitually wore or, apart from the obvious exception of 'Green', one's hair colouring or even complexion.

The surname Red developed into Reid, while

Blue was rare and no-one wanted to be associated with yellow.

Rather self-important individuals took surnames that include Goodman and Wiseman, while physical attributes crept into surnames such as Small and Little.

Many families proudly boast the heraldic device known as a Coat of Arms, as featured on our front cover.

The central motif of the Coat of Arms would originally have been what was borne on the shield of a warrior to distinguish himself from others on the battlefield.

Not featured on the Coat of Arms, but high-lighted on page three, is the family motto and related crest – with the latter frequently different from the central motif.

Adding further variety to the rich cultural heritage that is represented by surnames is the appearance in recent times in lists of the 100 most common names found in England of ones that include Khan, Patel and Singh – names that have proud roots in the vast sub-continent of India.

Echoes of a far distant past can still be found in our surnames and they can be borne with pride in commemoration of our forebears.

Chapter two:

Royal connections

**A name with a pedigree that stretches back
through the dim mists of time, 'Palmer' has been
present in the British Isles from the earliest times.**

In common with many other surnames found
today, however, it did not become popularised until
after the Norman Conquest of England in 1066.

First records of the name appear in Kent,
known as the 'Garden of England', but it was also to
be found in other geographical locations in what are
now some redundant spelling forms such as 'Palmere.'

It is in this form that the name is recorded in
Kent in 1086, twenty years after the Conquest, while
Ralph de Palmere appears much further north, in
Yorkshire, in 1273 and a Roger le Palmere is recorded
in Middlesex in 1440.

Derived from the Old French 'paulmer' or
'palmer', in turn derived from the Latin 'palmifer',
the name originally meant 'palm bearer' and indicated
Christian pilgrims to the Holy Land who, to prove
they had made the arduous journey, would bring back
a palm branch.

With the palm a symbol of triumph and victory even before Christian times – with the Romans, for example, rewarding military heroes with symbolic palm branches – it became a pre-eminent Christian symbol of the victory of the faithful following Jesus's triumphal entry into Jerusalem.

Now celebrated on the Sunday before Easter as Palm Sunday, it commemorates how the faithful laid down palm leaves in the path of Jesus as he made his way into the Holy City.

In medieval times there was a lucrative trade in spurious religious relics, such as slivers of wood that were claimed to have come from the True Cross on which Jesus was crucified.

So widespread was this trade, with incredulous numbers of the faithful buying up these so-called relics that 'palmer' also became a nickname for someone who dealt in such 'relics.'

But it is far from their original connection to Christian pilgrims and missionaries or dealers in holy relics that bearers of the Palmer name enter the often turbulent historical record of England.

As part of the high romance and drama that is this history, one couple of the name stamped a particularly colourful mark on the record.

They were Roger Palmer, 1st Earl of Castlemaine and his wife Barbara, the most notorious of the many mistresses of Charles II and who was also commonly known by her maiden name of Barbara Villiers.

Born in 1634, the son of Sir James Palmer, a Gentleman of the Bedchamber of the ill-fated Stuart monarch Charles I and Catherine Herbert, daughter of William Herbert, 1st Baron Powis, the devout Roman Catholic became a noted courtier, politician and diplomat.

In 1659 he married the 19-year-old Barbara Villiers, born in Westminster, London and a daughter of William Villiers, 2nd Viscount Grandison.

It was while Charles II was still in exile in The Hague that Palmer and his wife visited his court-in-exile and the vivacious Barbara became his mistress shortly afterwards.

One reason that has been advanced as to why her husband should have acquiesced to this is that it may have been because of his almost blind devotion to the Stuart monarchy.

Following the Restoration of Charles II in 1660, the monarch rewarded his highly favoured mistress by creating her husband Baron Limerick and

1st Earl of Castlemaine, with Barbara becoming Countess of Castlemaine and, later, also 1st Duchess of Cleveland.

Described by one source as having been "tall, voluptuous, with masses of auburn hair, slanting, heavy-lidded blue-violet eyes, alabaster skin, and a sensuous, silky mouth", her influence over the king became so great that she was referred to as "The Uncrowned Queen."

But less complimentary contemporary accounts describe her as "the curse of the nation" because of her "extravagance, foul temper and promiscuity."

Following the death of Charles II in 1685 and the accession to the throne of James II (James VII of Scotland), the Earl of Castlemaine was appointed to the English Privy Council and later as Ambassador to the Vatican.

But the fortunes of both he and his by now estranged wife were all but destroyed in the wake of what is known as the Glorious Revolution of 1688 that saw the flight into exile of James – the last of the Stuart monarchs – and the accession to the throne of the Protestant William of Orange and his wife Mary.

In common with many other influential

figures who had been prominent in their support of the Stuart monarchy, the 1st Earl of Castlemaine was confined for a time in the Tower of London.

Released after spending several months in the Tower, he died in 1705, while Barbara died four years later.

She was the mother of five children fathered by Charles II: all recognised and ennobled by him, they included Lady Anne Palmer, later Lady Anne Fitzroy, and Charles Palmer who was created Duke of Southampton in 1675.

The colourful live and times of the Countess of Castlemaine form the subject of a number of plays and novels that include George Bernard Shaw's *In Good King Charles's Golden Age*, Kathleen Windsor's 1944 book *Forever Amber* and Patricia Campbell Horton's 1977 *Royal Mistress*.

In a later century Roundell Palmer was the British lawyer and politician who achieved high office and was honoured with a number of titles in the Peerage of the United Kingdom.

Born in 1812 in Mixbury, Oxfordshire, the son of a parish rector, he studied at Oxford University and was later called to the bar.

Entering Parliament in 1847 as a Conservative,

he later joined the breakaway faction of the party that in 1859 helped to create what became the Liberal Party.

Serving as Solicitor General between 1861 and 1863 and as Attorney General between 1863 and 1866, he was ennobled as Baron Selborne following his appointment as Lord Chancellor of Great Britain in 1872.

It was in his role of Lord Chancellor that he was responsible for the passage of the Judiciary Act of 1873 that radically overhauled the judicial system.

Serving again as Lord Chancellor from 1880 to 1885, he was created Viscount Wolmer and, later, 1st Earl of Selborne.

Having broken with the Liberal Party in 1885 and joining the Liberal Unionists over his opposition to proposals for Irish Home Rule, he died in 1895.

He was the father of the politician and colonial administrator William Waldegrave Palmer, 2nd Earl of Selborne.

Born in 1859, he served from 1882 to 1885 as assistant private secretary to Hugh Childers, Chancellor of the Exchequer, before being elected to Parliament as the Liberal member for East Hampshire.

In common with his father, he broke with the Liberals over the issue of Home Rule and joined the Liberal Unionists.

Subsequently holding an impressive number of high level Government posts that included Under-Secretary of State for the Colonies, First Lord of the Admiralty, High Commissioner for South Africa and, during the First World War, President of the Board of Agriculture, he died in 1942.

Also in politics, but far removed from British shores, Sir Geoffrey Palmer, born in 1942, served, as leader of the Labour Party, from August of 1989 until September of 1990 as 33rd Prime Minister of New Zealand.

Chapter three:

Fame and infamy

Bearers of the Palmer name have also stamped their mark on the historical record as highly successful entrepreneurs.

Born in 1818 in Long Sutton, Somerset, George Palmer is credited as having been primarily instrumental in the success of the biscuit company whose famous brand of Huntley and Palmer is internationally recognised to this day.

It was in 1822 that Joseph Huntley founded a small biscuit maker and confectioner shop known as J. Huntley and Son in London Street, Reading, in Berkshire.

Selling his biscuits mainly to stage coach travellers who stopped off at a coaching inn across the road from his premises, he later expanded his business to include the manufacture of biscuits tins to avoid breakage of his popular culinary delights.

Ill-health forced him to retire in 1838, passing over control of the business to his son Thomas who, three years later, took his distant cousin George Palmer on as a business partner.

Palmer soon became the dominant partner in the enterprise, overseeing the manufacture of its products from much larger premises in Reading's Kings Road.

Thomas Huntley died in 1857 and Palmer, later aided by his sons William and Samuel, expanded and promoted the business to the extent that, now known as Huntley and Palmer, it became under Royal Warrant biscuit makers to the Royal Family.

Utilising innovative methods of mass production and employing more than 5,000 people by 1900, the company was the world's largest biscuit firm – producing more than 400 different varieties by 1903.

So identified with Reading did Huntley and Palmer become that the town became known as "biscuit town", and the local football club as "the biscuit men."

The Palmers were also generous benefactors of the town – gifting it, for example, the land known as Palmer Park.

George Palmer had died in 1897, but the business continued to prosper under his descendants.

Various changes of ownership have ensued over the years and manufacturing ended in Reading in 1976; owned since 2008 by the Freeman family,

Huntley and Palmer now operates from Sudbury, in Suffolk.

One of George Palmer's descendants is Adrian Palmer, 4th Baronet Palmer, the aristocrat and landowner in Scotland born in 1951.

At the time of writing one of the ninety hereditary peers to sit in the House of Lords, as a young man he worked for a time in the family's biscuit factory in Reading.

Working as their sales manager in Belgium and Luxembourg in the early 1970s, he later, from 1977 to 1986, was the Scottish representative to the European Landowners' Organisation.

Many other posts he has held include membership from 1986 to 1992 of the Scottish Landowners' Federation and chairman of the Country Sports Defence Trust.

Born in 1822 in South Shields, Sir Charles Palmer was not only a Liberal Party politician but also a noted nineteenth century coal-mining entrepreneur and shipbuilder.

Owner of a number of collieries in the north-east of England, he established shipbuilding yards at Jarrow, on the Tyne, that included steelworks and rolling mills.

Having set up the company of Palmer's Shipbuilding and Iron Company in 1865, he died in 1907, having been raised to the Peerage as 1st Baronet of Grinkle Park and Newcastle-upon-Tyne.

Born in 1838 in Bangalore, in what was then British India, Major-General Henry Palmer is noted for having developed, in his capacity as a foreign advisor to the Empire of Japan, Yokohama Harbour.

The son of a British colonel in the Madras Army and being commissioned as a lieutenant in the Royal Engineers in 1856 after studying at the Royal Military Academy, Woolwich, he was later assigned to British Columbia, Canada.

This was when, as part of a survey mission, he supervised major road construction.

Serving from 1864 to 1874 with the Ordnance Survey of Great Britain, it was after he retired from the Royal Engineers in 1887 that he was hired by the Japanese government to develop designs for both harbour and city waterworks.

It was in this capacity that he designed Yokohama harbour before his death in 1893, while a bronze bust of Palmer was unveiled by the Yokohama Water Works in 1987.

Bearers of the Palmer name have also been innovators in the field of medicine.

Born in 1845 in Pickering, Ontario but later moving to the United States, Daniel David Palmer, better known as D.D. Palmer, was the founder of the medical technique known as chiropractic.

It was after settling in Davenport, Iowa as a practitioner of what was then known as magnetic healing that in 1895 he cured a man's healing impairment by what became known as the technique of chiropractic.

This technique, according to Palmer, could cure what he termed 'dis-ease' by the manipulation of the spinal column.

Opening the Palmer School of Chiropractic in Davenport in 1897, he died in 1913 after having passed his practice on to his son Bartlett Palmer, born in 1882 and who died in 1961.

On the field of battle Frederick Palmer was a recipient during the First World War of the Victoria Cross, the highest award for valour in the face of enemy action for British and Commonwealth forces.

Born in 1891 in Hammersmith, London, he had been a lance-sergeant in the 22nd Battalion, The Royal Fusiliers when in February of 1917 north of

Courcette, France, he managed to repel successive waves of heavy enemy attacks by rallying his men.

Serving as a Wing-Commander in the Royal Air Force during the Second World War, he died in 1955.

One particularly infamous bearer of the otherwise proud name of Palmer was the English medical doctor William Palmer – more notoriously known as "The Prince of Poisoners" or "The Rugeley Poisoner".

Born in 1824 in Rugeley, Staffordshire, he was publicly hanged in June of 1856 after a celebrated trial in which he was found guilty of the murder by poisoning for monetary gain of one of his friends, John Crook.

A heavy gambler and frequently in debt, Palmer was also suspected of having used his trusted position as a doctor to murder a number of other people who included four of his own infant children and his mother-in-law through poisoning either their food or drink.

Today's common salutation of "What's your poison?" when offering someone a drink is thought to have originally been a black-humoured reference to the evil deeds of Dr William Palmer.

His notorious crimes were the subject of the 1998 film *The Life and Crimes of William Palmer*, with actor Keith Allen in the role of Palmer.

On a decidedly more uplifting and honourable note, Orio Palmer was one of the heroes of the aftermath of the terrorist attack on New York's World Trade Center on September 11, 2001.

Born in 1956, he was a battalion chief of the New York City Fire Department when he led a crew of fire-fighters as far as the 78th floor of the Center's South Tower after it had been struck by a hijacked aircraft.

On their way to the 78th floor, Palmer and his crew conducted many people to safety down the stairwells before they themselves were killed when the tower collapsed.

The 9/11 Commission into the terrorist attack recorded that Palmer and his crew had played "an indispensable role in ensuring calm in the stairwells, assisting the injured and guiding the evacuees on the lower floors."

Palmer and his brave crew are now remembered on the National 9/11 Memorial.

Chapter four:

On the world stage

Born in 1914, Lilli Marie Pieser was the German actress better known by her stage name of Lilli Palmer.

The daughter of a German-Jewish surgeon and an Austrian-Jewish stage actress, she studied drama in Berlin before fleeing with her parents to France in 1933 following the Nazi Party's rise to power.

Appearing in cabaret in Paris, she attracted the attention of British film talent scouts, resulting in her being signed up to the Gaumont Film Company.

Her screen debut came in 1935 in *Crime Unlimited* while, after her marriage in 1943 to the actor Rex Harrison, she followed him to Hollywood and subsequently starred in a number of films that include the 1946 *Cloak and Dagger*, the 1947 *Body and Soul*, the 1963 *Miracle of the White Stallions* and the 1971 *Murders in the Rue Morgue*.

Also the star of a number of German-made films that include the 1958 *Müdchen in Uniform (Girls in Uniform)*, she was divorced from Rex Harrison in 1956.

Later marrying the Argentinean actor Carlos Thompson and a recipient of a star on the Hollywood Walk of Fame and the Great Cross of Merit of the Federal Republic of Germany, she died in 1986.

In contemporary times, Julie Anne Harris is the English television actress better known as **Patsy Palmer**.

Born in 1972 in Bethnal Green, London she first came to prominence on British television screens in the children's drama *Grange Hill*, but is much better known for her role of Bianca Jackson in the popular soap *EastEnders*.

This role won her the Best Actress Award at the 2000 British Soap Awards.

The recipient of an OBE for his services to drama, **Geoffrey Palmer** is the English actor born in London in 1927.

An actor of stage, radio, television and film, he is best known for his roles in a number of popular British television sitcoms that include *The Rise and Fall of Reginald Perrin*, *Butterflies* and *As Time Goes By*.

Big screen credits include the 1998 *A Fish Called Wanda* and, from 2009, *The Pink Panther 2*, while he has also narrated a number of audio books.

Born in New York City in 1976, **Amanda Palmer** is the singer, songwriter and pianist best known for having been a member, along with Brian Viglione, of the duo The Dresden Dolls.

Having enjoyed hits with The Dresden Dolls that include their 2002 self-titled album, she has also had success along with Jason Webb with the duo Evelyn Evelyn, and with the band Amanda Palmer and the Grand Theft Orchestra.

The recipient of two separate Grammy Awards for Best Male Rock Performance and nominated twice for the Brit Award for Best British Male, **Robert Palmer** was the English singer and songwriter born in 1949 in Batley, West Yorkshire.

Best known for a number of hits that most notably include *Addicted to Love* and *Simply Irresistible*, he died in 2003.

Behind the drum kit, **Carl Palmer** is the English drummer and percussionist born in 1950 in Handsworth, Birmingham.

Recognised as one of the world's top rock drummers, bands he has been a member of include The Crazy World of Arthur Brown, Atomic Rooster and Asia – but he is best known, along with Keith Emerson and Greg Lake, for having been a member of the 1970s' progressive rock band Emerson, Lake and Palmer.

One of the first session musicians to be inducted into the Rock and Roll Hall of Fame, **Earl Palmer** was the legendary rock and roll and rhythm and blues drummer who played for bands and artistes who include Fats Domino, Little Richard and Tom Waits.

Born in 1924 in New Orleans, he died in 2008.

In a much different musical genre Felicity Palmer, more properly known as **Dame Felicity Palmer**, is the English mezzo-soprano and music professor born in Cheltenham in 1944.

Having studied at the Guildhall School of Music and Drama in London and the Munich College for Music and Theatre, her operatic debut was in 1971 as Dido in a Kent Opera production of *Dido and Aeneas*.

Making her debut with English National Opera four years later, she is now a professor at the Royal College of Music in London.

The recipient of a CBE in 1993, she was made a Dame Commander of the British Empire (DBE) in 2011 for her services to music.

Bearers of the Palmer name have also excelled,

and continue to excel, in the highly competitive world of sport.

Recognised as one of the greatest players in the history of men's professional golf, **Arnold Palmer** was born in 1929 in Latrobe, Pennsylvania.

First taking up the golf clubs as a child under the tutelage of his father Milford Palmer, who was head professional and greens-keeper at Latrobe Country Club, he later served for a time in the U.S. Coast Guard.

Winner of the 1954 U.S. Amateur and turning professional, he went on to win the Canadian Open the following year.

This was the first of many major wins that include the Masters Tournament in 1958, 1960, 1962 and 1964 and the Professional Golfers Association (PGA) Championship in 1964, 1968 and 1970.

Nicknamed "The King" and highly respected by fellow golf professionals and golfing fans alike, along with Gary Player and Jack Nicklaus he is known as one of the game's "Big Three."

His many honours and accolades include induction into the World Golf Hall of fame and a PGA Lifetime Achievement Award.

Awarded the Presidential Medal of Freedom

by George W. Bush in 2004, he was awarded the equally prestigious Congressional Gold Medal five years later.

Arnold Palmer Regional Airport in his hometown of Latrobe is also named in his honour.

From golf to tennis, **Jared Palmer** was ranked in 2000 as the world's No.1 men's doubles player.

Born in 1971 in New York City and turning professional when he was aged 20, his many doubles' wins include the 1995 Australian Open and Wimbledon in 2001.

On the motor racing circuit **Jonathan Palmer**, born in London in 1956, is the entrepreneur and former driver whose wins include the 1981 British Formula Three Championship and the 1983 European Formula Two Championship.

A medical doctor and a former commentator on Formula 1 for the BBC, as a businessman he is involved in the operation of the British Brands Hatch, Oulton Park, Caldwell Park and Snetterton racing circuits.

From sport to art, **Garrick Palmer** is the internationally acclaimed English painter, wood engraver and photographer born in 1933 in Portsmouth.

A Fellow of the Royal Society of Painter-

Printmakers, his wood engravings have appeared in reissues of classic books by publishers who include the Folio Society.

With his photographs featured on stamps issued by Canada Post in 2003 and on Alberta's 2005 Centennial Stamp, **Harry Palmer** is the photographer born in 1930 in Calgary, Alberta.

Author of books that include his 1983 *Calgary Places and People* and the 1992 *125 Portraits*, many of his photographs are in the collection of Canada's Library and Archives.

In the equally creative world of the written word, **Michael Palmer** is the doctor and writer of best-selling medical thrillers that include his 1982 *The Sisterhood* and the 1991 *Extreme Measures* – adapted for a film of the same name in 1996.

Born in 1942 in Springfield, Massachusetts he has served as an associate director of the Massachusetts Medical Society's physician health programme.

Married to fellow children's author Theodor Seuss Geisel, better known by his pen-name of Dr Seuss, **Helen Palmer Geisel** was born in 1899 in Amherst, Massachusetts.

The author of popular books that include the

1963 *Do You Know What I'm Doing Next Saturday?* and the 1964 *Why I Built the Boogle House*, she took her own life in 1967 after suffering from a long series of illnesses.

One particularly colourful bearer of the proud name of Palmer was the American business-woman, socialite and philanthropist **Bertha Palmer**, described by her contemporaries as "beautiful, dashing, quick and smart."

Born Bertha Honoré in 1849 in Louisville Kentucky, the daughter of a wealthy businessman, she was aged 21 when she married the 44-year-old Chicago millionaire Potter Palmer.

Having built up a highly lucrative business selling a range of high quality goods, including the latest ladies' French fashions, to the elite of Chicago high society, he sold the business to a consortium shortly after his marriage and built the luxurious Palmer House Hotel.

The hotel was destroyed only a few months later in the Great Fire of Chicago of October 1871, while most of his other land holdings were also wiped out.

But through the business acumen of his young wife Bertha, the couple managed to restore their fortunes to the extent that they became ranked as among the richest people in the United States.

While Bertha became the most sought after hostess in Chicago, the couple also amassed a collection of Impressionist Paintings that included 29 Monets and 11 Renoirs.

Bertha also became a pioneer of real estate in Florida, while also travelling throughout Europe and dining with royalty, statesmen and industrialists.

The couple spent lavish sums on their Palmer Mansion in Chicago, mainly at the instigation of the free-spending Bertha.

When Potter Palmer dictated his will, he stipulated that should he pre-decease her, whoever married her next should be granted a large sum of money from his estate.

When asked why, he replied: "Because he'll need it."

He died in 1902, while Bertha never remarried.

She died in 1918, a generous benefactor of a number of charitable causes, while she and her husband's priceless collection of Impressionist Paintings now form an important part of the collection of the Art Institute of Chicago.